P9-BZZ-829

P9-BZZ-829

THE *FANTASTIC* BOOK OF

GYMNASTICS

LLOYD READHEAD

COPPER BEECH BOOKS
BROOKFIELD, CONNECTICUT

© Aladdin Books Ltd 1997
© U.S. text 1997

*Designed and
produced by*
Aladdin Books Ltd
28 Percy Street
London W1P 0LD

*First published in the United States
in 1997 by*
Copper Beech Books,
an imprint of
The Millbrook Press
2 Old New Milford Road
Brookfield, Connecticut 06804

Editor
Sarah Levete
Design
David West
Children's Book Design
Designer
Flick Killerby
Illustrator
Catherine Ward – Simon Girling &
Associates
Picture Research
Brooks Krikler Research

Printed in Belgium
All rights reserved
5 4 3 2 1

Library of Congress
Cataloging-in-Publication Data

Readhead, Lloyd.
Gymnastics / Lloyd Readhead ; illustrated by
Catherine Ward.
p. cm. — (The fantastic book of—)
Includes index.
Summary: Provides a look at artistic, rhythmic,
and sports gymnastics, the various positions and
moves involved, devising a routine, and more.
Includes fold-out pages on gymnastics
competitions.
ISBN 0-7613-0622-6 (lib. bdg.). —
ISBN 0-7613-0637-4 (trade hardcover) :
1. Gymnastics—Juvenile literature.
2. Gymnastics for children—Juvenile literature.
3. Toy and movable books—Specimens.
[1. Gymnastics. 2. Toy and movable books.]
I. Ward, Catherine, ill. II. Title. III. Series
GV461.R43 1997   97-10591
796.44—dc21   CIP AC

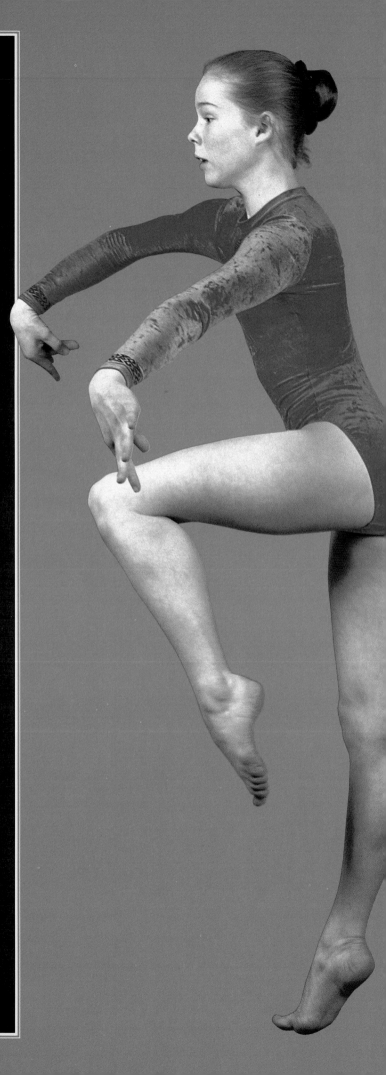

CONTENTS

THE FOLD-OUT SECTION

Introduction

Breathtaking to watch and exciting to
perform, gymnastics is one of the
most popular sports with both boys and
girls. The best gymnasts demonstrate amazing
skill, exceptional strength, and great courage – they
make even the most difficult movements look easy.

Gymnastics is an exciting and exhilarating
sport, but it can be dangerous if it is not practiced
correctly. Whatever your level, train under the
guidance of a qualified and experienced coach.

A young gymnast can begin his or her career in a
class at school or in a club. Then he or she may
compete in club, county, regional, and national
events. You may not reach the dizzying heights
of top gymnast Shannon Miller *(right)*,
competing for the Olympic Games, but you can
still enjoy gymnastics at any level, as a spectator
or participant.

This book takes you from the warm-up to basic
and advanced exercises in artistic gymnastics, the
most popular competitive discipline of this sport. A
key *(see page 39)* identifies the different apparatus
used by boys and girls. There are also chapters on
rhythmic gymnastics and sports acrobatics.

An eight-page fold-out leads you inside the world
of top-level competitive gymnastics, showing you
what goes on behind the scenes and in front of the
cameras, from the training to the judging.

Gymnastics is challenging and demanding, but if
you are prepared to make the effort, you will find it
rewarding and fun.

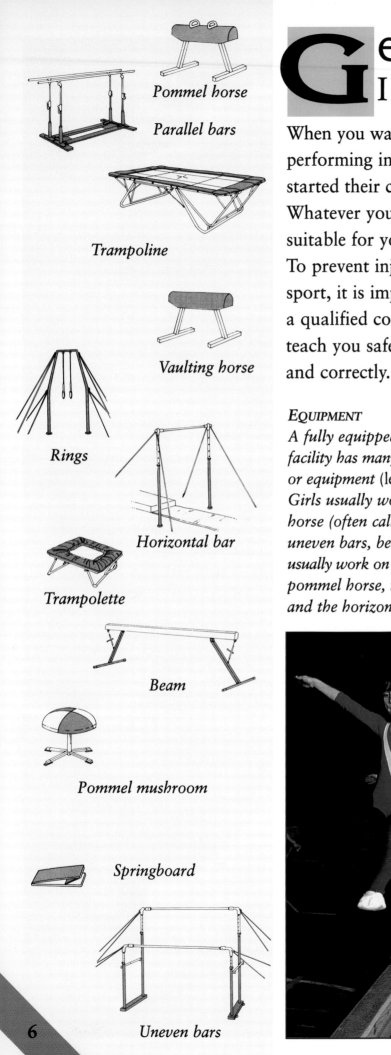

Pommel horse

Parallel bars

Trampoline

Vaulting horse

Rings

Horizontal bar

Trampolette

Beam

Pommel mushroom

Springboard

Uneven bars

Getting started
IN GYMNASTICS

When you watch television and see the top gymnasts performing incredible exercises, remember that they all started their careers with a basic gymnastics class! Whatever your ability and age, there will be a class suitable for you, either at school or in a gymnastics club. To prevent injury and to make the most of the sport, it is important that you are taught by a qualified coach or teacher who can teach you safely and correctly.

EQUIPMENT
A fully equipped gymnastics training facility has many pieces of apparatus or equipment (left) and safety mats. Girls usually work on the vaulting horse (often called the vault), uneven bars, beam, and floor. Boys usually work on the floor, the pommel horse, the rings, the vault, and the horizontal and parallel bars.

SCHOOLS
For many young people, their first taste of gymnastics is during physical education classes at school (*left*). Students are taught simple movement patterns and basic gymnastics by a gym teacher. Those with more ability or greater interest can learn more by joining an after-school gymnastics class.

JOINING A CLUB

If you enjoy gymnastics at school, why not join a local, recognized gymnastics club (below)? Your school may have connections with a local club. Before joining, ask to look around the gym – check too that the gym is safe and well-equipped. Ask if you can watch a training session.

INSPIRATION

Many young people (and sometimes their parents too!) are inspired to join a gymnastics club after they have seen superstars, such as Shannon Miller *(right)*, on the television.

Top gymnasts reach the peak of their careers through hard work and talent – but remember, you don't have to score a perfect 10 to enjoy gymnastics!

COACHING

As well as looking after your safety and well-being, your coach will identify your strengths and weaknesses.

In considering these, he or she will design a program to help you learn and develop to the best of your abilities. It takes great determination and dedication to become a successful gymnast – a good coach will try to develop these characteristics, as well as supervise your physical training. Your coach will also try to motivate you by offering frequent encouragement.

HISTORY OF GYMNASTICS

The word "gymnast" was first used to describe the naked athletes who performed gymnastics movements in the ancient Greek and Roman civilizations.

During the Middle Ages only acrobats *(left)* performed gymnastics, but in the late 18th century people began to recognize the benefits of physical activity *(right)* on the body and mind. A German schoolteacher, Friedrich Jahn (1778-1852), built the first modern gymnastics equipment. The military adopted this to help keep soldiers fit and strong.

Men's artistic gymnastics *(see pages 26-27)* has been featured in the Olympic Games since 1896. It was only in 1928 that women were allowed to compete.

MUSCLES

Your limbs move when your brain sends a message to a particular muscle group. As one muscle contracts or tightens, it pulls on the bones in your limbs to make them move. As the muscle on one side of the limb contracts, the muscle on the other side relaxes. Stretching your muscles will improve flexibility in your joints – the point where two bones meet. To prevent injury, stretch your muscles gradually.

LOWER LEG STRETCH
To stretch your back muscles and the back of your lower legs start in a squat position. Gently lean forward, and alternately stretch each leg back.

W arm-up
EXERCISES

Before starting any form of gymnastics activity, it is essential that you have a "warm-up" period. During this, your muscles gradually "warm-up" as the blood flow to them increases. This reduces the risk of injury when you begin more strenuous gymnastics exercises. Your heart, lungs, and muscles also work better as your body warms up.

SHOULDER STRETCH
To stretch your shoulders, your coach or partner can work with you to apply gentle force on your upper arms (right).

This exercise (right) stretches your lower back, hip, and thigh muscles. It is often used in the warm-up. Press your elbow against your opposite, raised, thigh; rotate or turn your shoulders in the direction of your bent leg.

GETTING WARMER!

To make sure that your body heat is not wasted, wear a sweatshirt or T-shirt and sweatpants *(far right)* during the first stages of the warm-up. After this, girls wear a leotard. Boys wear a leotard and shorts. Begin your warm-up with gentle but physical games, which can be fun too! As you get warmer, add more energetic exercises such as jogging. You are now ready to stretch.

WRISTS AND ANKLES

In gymnastics, wrist and ankle joints are put under a lot of stress. Stretch your wrists by kneeling with your arms straight. Press your hands into the floor; keep your weight forward *(above)*. To stretch your ankles, ask a partner to hold lightly above your knees and to press down gently on the top of your feet *(below)*.

REMEMBER:
Train only
under the
supervision of a
qualified coach.

STRETCHING SLOWLY

Stretch slowly, otherwise you may injure yourself by "pulling" a muscle. Never force a stretch and never "bounce." You can give your muscles a good stretch by holding the final position for a few seconds. Your coach may add specific warm-up exercises if you are going to concentrate on a particular piece of apparatus.

This exercise will help gradually to arch your back. Keep your hands pressed onto the floor and your stomach pulled in to help protect your lower back.

TAKE CARE OF YOUR BACK
Stretch your spine with a gentle sideways bend. Bend your upper body in a straight line over your hips, extending your top arm (right). Repeat for both sides. It is important not to place too much strain on your spine, particularly in the lower back.

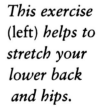

This exercise (left) helps to stretch your lower back and hips.

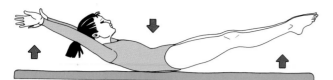

Dish

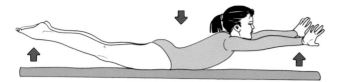

Arch

DISH AND ARCH

First practice these moves with bent legs, before advancing to straight legs. In the dish, press your lower back into the floor – tighten your stomach muscles to hold the slightly curved shape. In the arch, tighten your back and upper leg muscles to hold the hollow shape.

OTHER SPORTS

Many of the world's top sports coaches think that gymnastics is the best preparation and training for all athletic activities. Not only does it increase your fitness, flexibility, and strength, but it also teaches you moves such as somersaults and twists, which you can include in other sports, from diving *(right)* to snowboarding.

BODY SHAPES

The key to many gymnastics moves is the ability to create and hold good body shapes *(above and right)*. To hold the required shapes, you need to develop good flexibility (the range of movement in your body) and strength to support your own body.

STRADDLE SIT

You will use this basic gymnastics shape in many other moves and routines. There are many variations on the straddle position. To perform the basic straddle sit (left) you need to be flexible in your hip joints. Keep your lower back straight.

CRADLE ROLL

In the cradle roll *(right)* the gymnast rocks forward and backward in the tucked position to gain the sensation that will be experienced in the forward and backward roll *(see pages 31-32)*. Keep your knees in close to your chest, and your head in a tucked position.

The first STEPS

From the bridge to the straddle sit, there are some basic gymnastics positions and techniques that you must learn before attempting more advanced skills. These first steps will help to develop your fitness, strength, and flexibility *(see pages 12-13)*, essential for a gymnast.

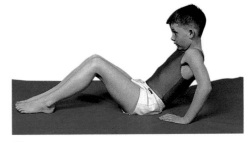

FALLING SAFELY
Falling safely can help you avoid injury. If you fall forward, point your fingers forward and bend your arms to soften the fall. If you fall backward (above), place your hands behind your body with your fingers pointing forward. Bend your arms and tuck your head in.

Learn these positions on the floor before using them on different pieces of apparatus.

The tuck position (left) is used in the forward and backward roll, as well as in the front and backward somersaults.

BRIDGE

Lie on a mat with your knees bent and your feet close to your body. With your fingers facing forward, place your hands behind you. Straighten your arms and legs as you push up. Keep your head between your arms. A flexible bridge *(right)* will help you later when you learn more advanced moves such as the backflip *(see page 33)*.

There should be a gradual curve of the spine.

LANDINGS
You need to know how to land well. It is worth practicing your landing technique many times – a poor landing can mean lost points in competition. The technique is important, whether you are landing from a jump (right) or from a piece of apparatus.

Land on the balls of your feet first; then quickly lower your heels and bend your knees and hips to absorb the force of the landing. Your heels stay on the floor until you are stationary and have straightened your legs.

Training: strength
AND FLEXIBILITY

As you increase the range of your gymnastics moves you will also need to improve your flexibility and strength. Flexibility is the range of movement in a particular muscle group or joint. Your flexibility training should be gentle and slow, with the final position held for more than six seconds.

Strength training exercises are used to improve the strength of the muscle groups that you use in a particular movement. This helps to improve the endurance of your muscles – the number of times you will be able to repeat a set of movements before becoming tired.

BODY TENSION EXERCISES
In these exercises you contract particular muscles without changing shape. The gymnast (above) is contracting his back, stomach, and leg muscles. These exercises improve your strength and will help you to hold body tension in advanced moves.

The lumbar fold helps develop flexibility in the hips and lower back (right). Tense your thigh muscles to keep your legs straight. Fold your upper body over to rest your chest on your thighs.

BURPEE JUMPS
Start in front support $\boxed{1}$; quickly squat to a crouch $\boxed{2}$; then explode into a vertical jump $\boxed{3}$. On landing in the squat $\boxed{4}$, extend to the front support position $\boxed{5}$, and repeat the exercise.

BALLET EXERCISES

Many gymnasts use classical ballet exercises in training. These controlled exercises help to develop flexibility and strength.

You will also often see different ballet positions and dance movements used in routines – particularly in Women's Artistic Gymnastics, Rhythmic Gymnastics, and Sports Acrobatics.

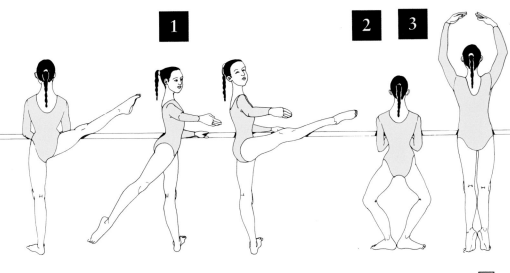

Classical ballet exercises such as leg swings 1 *, the demi-plié* 2 *, and the relevé* 3 *will improve your posture and strength.*

BOX SPLITS

Box splits are performed with the legs to the side of the body and with the legs flat to the floor. Lay your chest flat on the floor or sit upright *(right)*. Both the box splits and the front splits, where you face the direction of your leading leg, will help develop flexibility in your hips.

Repeating a sequence of burpee jumps will help improve your strength.

HEALTHY EATING

Gymnastics activity places huge demands on your body. Look after your body by eating balanced meals of carbohydrates (found in bread, potatoes, rice, and pasta), protein (found in meat, fish, eggs, milk, and legumes), and vitamins (found in fresh fruit and vegetables). You need a healthy body to perform at your best.

13

Women's artistic GYMNASTICS

In artistic gymnastics, women work on four pieces of apparatus – the uneven bars, the beam, the floor, and the vault. This discipline of gymnastics combines elegance with demanding balance skills and complex moves including many twists, springs, and rotations.

Although you can begin your training at an early age, you have to be sixteen years old before you can compete in major senior events.

What to wear
In competition, wear a leotard (left), which can be of any design. Choose a style that will be comfortable and unrestrictive.

VAULTING
Girls approach the side of the horse (the body of the vault); boys approach the end of the horse. For girls the vault's height is 48 in; for boys it is 54 in. All vaults are 64 in long and 14 in wide.

A routine on the vault *(below)* may include: a powerful run-up ⑴ ; a prejump ⑵ ; a takeoff from the springboard (of approximately 0.2 second); a first flight ⑶ ; a thrust from the hands ⑷ ; a second flight ⑸ ; and a controlled landing ⑹ . In the second flight you can introduce twists and somersaults before the landing. The photograph *(above right)* shows Dominique Dawes, USA, holding a good body position in mid-air, from her second flight on the vault.

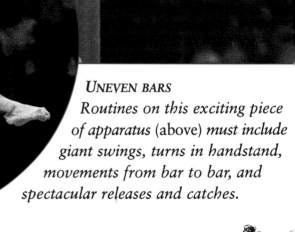

Uneven bars
Routines on this exciting piece of apparatus (above) must include giant swings, turns in handstand, movements from bar to bar, and spectacular releases and catches.

1   2   3

14

RISING STARS

In 1972, Olga Korbut, from the former Soviet Union, won the hearts of millions during her performances at the Munich Olympics in Germany. Among today's top female gymnasts is Ukrainian Lilia Podkopayeva *(right)*. She is noted for her forward tumbling work, and has won titles in both World European and Olympic Championships.

FLOOR EXERCISES

Both you and your gymnast need great skill in designing an attractive and challenging routine (see pages 36-37). It must show off your skills in only 70-90 seconds and use the music to the best effect. On the floor, include a variety of forward and backward tumbles, linked together by flowing, choreographed movements. You must also perform a series of leaps and spins and show the full range of your body movements.

BEAM

This is perhaps the most difficult of all apparatus for girls *(below)*, requiring great courage and precision in performance. The top gymnasts present amazing combinations of tumbles on the beam (only 5 inches wide), linked with balance and strength skills. It takes hours of practice to develop confidence and skill on the beam.

DISMOUNTS

You need to consider the dismount and landing *(see page 11)* as important as the exercises or routine performed on the apparatus. Your routine must end with a dismount that matches the difficulty rating *(see page 23)* of the full routine. For instance, a dismount from the uneven bars usually includes two somersaults or twists. Your landing must look controlled and be carried out without any hops, steps, or unsteadiness.

4
5
6

Rhythmic GYMNASTICS

This discipline of gymnastics is for females only. For a flowing performance, you need to be graceful and elegant as well as extremely flexible and strong. A rhythmic gymnast has to hold her limbs in incredible positions while throwing and catching a ball, a hoop, clubs, ribbon, or rope.

Although each piece of apparatus is very different to handle and to catch, you must be able to perform well with them all – four of the five pieces of apparatus are nominated annually to be used in competition.

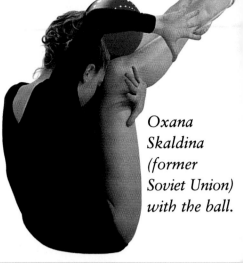

Oxana Skaldina (former Soviet Union) with the ball.

IN COMPETITION
In the individual competition each gymnast performs a routine set to music with each of the four nominated pieces of apparatus. Medals are presented for the best performance in each event as well as for the gymnast with the highest combined total.

CLUBS
In one or both hands, the rhythmic gymnast must throw, catch, and manipulate the clubs while she performs other movements, as shown by Russian Armina Zaripova.

RIBBONS AND HOOP
Adriona Dunavska (Bulgaria) creates shapes with the ribbon (above), *and Marina Lobach (former Soviet Union) holds the standing splits with the hoop* (right).

16

Qualifying

SELECTION
Around the world, national coaches watch the progress and potential of young gymnasts. The more talented will be selected for special training within the National Squad system. The selectors monitor the young gymnasts' progress *(center)* over a series of progressively more demanding events. They look for gymnasts who achieve high scores and who can compete with determination.

The 1996 Chinese men's Olympic team and coaches.

STARTING YOUNG
Very young gymnasts begin to compete in club competitions, gradually progressing to county, regional, national, and international group events.

THE OLYMPIC TEAM Coaches select up to twelve gymnasts to train for a year before selecting up to eight men and eight women for the national team.

COMPETITION LEVELS
Around the world, the most talented and committed gymnasts may have a chance to compete as individuals or team members in international events from the Commonwealth Games to the World Championships and, of course, the Olympic Games *(above)*.

PREPARATION
During the last weeks of training (above) before a competition, the gymnast focuses on his or her full competition routines in order to develop consistency and fitness. He or she must also prepare mentally to cope with the intense pressure of performing in a competition.

THE ARENA

The judges are seated in the aisles around the podium. The podium is set up with a mat for floor work [1] *; vaulting horses for men and women* [2] *; a pommel horse* [3] *; bars (parallel, horizontal, and uneven)* [4] *; balance beam* [5] *; and rings* [6] *.*

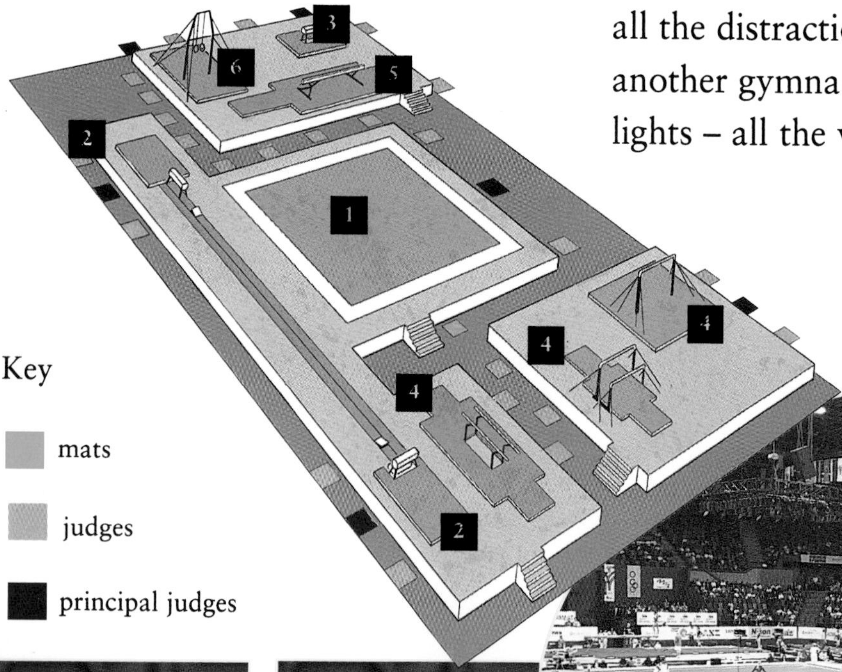

Key

mats

judges

principal judges

THE ARENA

When the men have completed their exercises, the podium is set up with apparatus for the women's competition. Each competitor must try to block out all the distractions in the arena, from applause for another gymnast to the intense television camera lights – all the while performing his or her best.

Lilia Podkopayeva (above and right) shows flair and originality.

All-around COMPETITION

The top 36 men and top 24 women in the team event qualify to compete again in the all-around competition. Each gymnast competes on all the pieces of apparatus. The individual who achieves the highest total score is the all-around winner.

Competition Events

Major COMPETITIONS

At top international gymnastics competitions such as the Olympic Games, the World Championships, the World Cup, and the European Championships there are three sections in the Men's and Women's artistic competitions: a team competition; an individual all-around competition; and individual apparatus finals. In each of these elements, the men perform on six pieces of apparatus (*see page 26*) and the women on four (*see page 14*). After the pre-competition warm-up, the gymnasts march into the arena behind their national flag. They line up in front of the judges before the competition begins.

READY, SET, GO!
The judges show the gymnast a green light, to signal that they are ready. The competitor then raises his or her right arm to show that the exercise will begin. Daisuke Nishikawa from Japan (left) checks that the parallel bars are ready for his performance.

Judges look for excellent technique (left).

Team COMPETITION

The first element of a competition is the team event for men and women. A maximum of six team members work on each apparatus. The top five scores on each apparatus are added up to provide the team total. This determines the team ranking – the order in which the team is placed according to their scores.

K. Mizushima (Japan) shows skill on the pommel horse.

Behind the Scenes

SETTING UP

Preparation for a major competition begins two years before the actual event. In the final week the activity in the main arena is hectic – the podium is erected and the apparatus is assembled. The electronic scoring system and the public address system are installed and tested. Three days before the opening, the gymnasts rehearse in the arena in a "podium" session to accustom them to the noise and lights.

150 female & 150 male competitors

WHO'S WHO?
In a major event there are hundreds of people involved (right), *from an arena organizer to a general team of medics.*

50 male & 50 female judges – a B jury of six judges for each event

LIGHTS, CAMERA, ACTION!
Two days before the event, television engineers install miles of cables, numerous lights, and cameras. Rehearsals take place during the podium session to ensure that the cameras can move

Chinese Li Xiaoshiang watches from the side.

TRAINING THE JUDGES
At a major event, all the judges *(left)* will attend a judging course at the venue to ensure that they are able to fulfill the responsible task of judging fairly.

An A jury (two expert judges) for each event

They will also watch the gymnasts' training sessions to take note of any new skills or moves that the competitors may use in their routine.

Competition Rules

SCORING

After watching each exercise the A jury gives a "start value," based on difficulty rating and including the special requirements *(see below)*. The B jury deducts points for poor form and errors. The highest and lowest of these scores are discounted – the other four are averaged. This value is then subtracted from the start value to give the final score.

Two coaches with each team

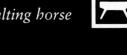
Floor

Uneven bars

Rings

Pommel horse

Parallel bars

Beam

Horizontal bar

Vaulting horse

JUDGING PRINCIPLES

The difficulty ratings are: A = simple; B = less simple; C = difficult; D = more difficult; E = very difficult; Super E = extremely difficult. A routine must include at least 1D, 2C, 3B, 4A elements, and 3 special requirements that prove a gymnast's range of skills on a piece of apparatus. Bonus points are given for difficult elements; deductions are made for errors such as bending the legs (above).

Each team has its own doctor (above) and physiotherapist (below).

ONE LANGUAGE

A symbol (above) represents each piece of apparatus on the electronic scoreboard, in the competition program, and on the judges' score cards.

FINAL SCORES

The medal presentation is spectacular, with the gymnasts marching onto the podium to the accompaniment of music. The champions are presented with the medals, and the national anthems of the winners are played. After the medal presentation the gymnasts parade around the arena and receive the applause that they richly deserve.

Vault medalists at the Atlanta Olympic Games, 1996

Individual APPARATUS FINAL

The top eight gymnasts on each apparatus in the team event qualify to compete again in the individual apparatus final. The competition order is determined by the drawing of lots. The gymnast who gains the highest score for his or her routine becomes the champion on that piece of apparatus.

PRESENTATION

As well as performing a demanding and skillful routine *(above)*, the gymnast must present himself or herself with confidence, elegance, and grace to the judges, as shown *(right)* by Dominique Dawes (USA). Even if the performance falters, the gymnast must continue the routine with composure.

Grigori Misutin (former Soviet Union) on the horizontal bar.

SPORTING BEHAVIOR
Every gymnast will compete hard for the best results. At the end of the event, there is always great respect and friendship shown among the participants. Sporting behavior, shown left by Shannon Miller and Lu Li (China), is an ever-present quality and feature of gymnastics.

END OF THE DAY
The climax of the day is the medal presentation to the winning gymnast or team. However, members of all teams will experience the excitement and tension of such a demanding event. Here, the British women's team support and congratulate each other during the 1995 World Championships.

You & your coach

TRAINING SCHEDULE phase: *competition* Date: Name:

day	load	warm up	physical prep					physical prep	warm down
Mon	medium	✔	choreo	(x8)	FX(x4)	FX(x4)	FX(x2)	endura	✔
Tues	light	✔	strength		1/2(x4)	1/2(x4)	1/2(x2)	flex	✔
Weds	heavy	✔		(x8)	FX(x5)	FX(x5)	FX(x3)		✔
Thurs	light	✔	choreo	(x8)	elem	elem	elem	specific strength	✔
Fri	rest	✔	rest	rest	rest	rest	rest	rest	✔
Sat	heavy	✔		(x8)	FX(x5)	FX(x5)	FX(x3)		✔
Sun	light	✔	specific strength	(x4)	FX(x1)	FX(x1)	FX(x1)	strength	✔

key: FX= full exercise 1/2= half exercise   (x2)=repeat twice elem=single elements   choreo=choreography endura=endurance

WORKING TOGETHER

You and your coach will spend a lot of time together. You will form a strong, trusting bond. He or she will try to understand your personality, your needs, and your particular characteristics. This will help your coach to guide you to your best level of performance.

TRAINING SCHEDULE

A planned training schedule (*left*) is essential to the successful development of a gymnast. The program for the year will be split into training phases, each phase carefully planned to bring the gymnast to peak performance for the main competition. The schedule will be designed to suit the stage of preparation, but the coach will ensure that the daily load is varied. A top gymnast may train two or three times a day for up to 30 hours per week.

Romanian coach Octavian Belu with gymnast Gina Gogean (left).

TRUST

As you gain experience, you will learn to trust your coach's judgment in all aspects of your training and participation in competitions. You will develop confidence in his or her ability to "spot" or support you while you learn demanding new skills (above).

TEAMWORK
The coach encourages the gymnasts and helps to keep them calm and focused. Even if his or her team members do not perform as well as expected, the coach must not show any sign of disappointment. He or she must remain positive and supportive of the team the whole time.

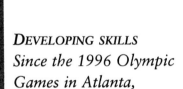

John Macready competes for the USA.

DEVELOPING SKILLS
Since the 1996 Olympic Games in Atlanta, competitors no longer have to perform compulsory exercises. The freedom to perform optional exercises allows each gymnast to develop new skills (left).

TUMBLING

On a 27-yard (25-meter) long springy track, the sports acrobat performs three tumbling routines: one with backward moves; one with twists; and one with backward and forward tumbles.

Sports ACROBATICS

There are now many clubs that specialize in this popular sport. In order to be successful as a sports acrobat you need to have good strength and very good balancing, leaping, and jumping skills. Both boys and girls can perform the tumbling work, the pairs work *(far right)*, and the group work *(center)*.

The top (supported partner)

The base (supporter)

BALANCE AND TEMPO

In the pairs and groups events the acrobats perform three different routines. The balance routine consists of a series of spectacular and unusual supported balance movements linked with dance and choreography as shown by Lyndsey Peters, Katie Lawton, and Nicola Wass, UK, (left). The tempo routine includes elements where one acrobat is thrown in the air to perform somersaults and twists before being recaught by his or her partner or partners.

IN COMPETITION

Apart from the men's group balance routine, the pairs and groups exercises are performed to music. Judges deduct points if they think that the music is not suitable for the routine. The picture shows Eugeny Marchento take the weight of Natalia Miller (both from the former Soviet Union), in one hand.

25

Men's artistic GYMNASTICS

In artistic gymnastics men work on six pieces of apparatus – the floor, the pommel horse, the rings, the vault, and the horizontal and parallel bars. Each event places different and huge strength demands on the gymnast – he may not be able to perform some of the elements until his body is fully developed at about eighteen years of age. Top gymnasts train for about thirty hours a week to develop the strength required.

RINGS
When you work on the rings (above) the force on your hands can be more than eight times your body weight! The rings, 9 feet (275 cm) above floor level, are 7 inches (18 cm) in diameter.

PARALLEL BARS

The parallel bars were first invented to develop gymnasts' strength for the pommel horse – today they are very popular with all gymnasts. The width of the bars can be adjusted to suit the individual.

A typical routine includes hangs 1 ; swings 2 ; movements where you release one or both hands and then regrasp the bar 3 ; balances held for 0.2 second 4 ; and dismounts 5 . Top gymnasts include multiple somersaults on the bars or as a dismount. Although there is no time limit for a routine in competition, most last for about 20 seconds.

STRADDLE NO MORE!
Unless a key part of the move, legs must not be straddled. The move (left) by Vladimir Artemov is no longer allowed.

WHAT TO WEAR
For the floor exercises and vaults you must wear a leotard and shorts (left). You can perform in bare feet or with gymnastic shoes to provide grip on takeoff and landings. On all other apparatus men must wear long sweatpants of a single color and socks together with a leotard (right), which may be multicolored.

26

FLOOR

For men, the floor exercise on a 14-square-foot (12 square-meter) springy base is not performed to music. Men should include a series of powerful forward and backward tumbles that include multiple somersaults and twists. Strength and flexibility should be demonstrated, as shown in the Japana fold *(see page 29)* performed by Cuban Sergio Suarez *(right)*.

A single leg swing on the demanding pommel horse

POMMEL HORSE

Many gymnasts and coaches believe that the pommel horse (a vaulting horse with handles attached) is the most difficult event. In competition you are only allowed one attempt at this – consistency and concentration are important factors. Apart from your hands, at no time during the routine can you touch the apparatus. As well as including circles of both legs, the routine must also feature scissor movements. Movements are performed on both handles, on one handle, and on the body of the horse.

RISING STARS
After many frustrating competitions as a junior gymnast when he made major mistakes in important events, Aleksei Nemov (Russia) has now developed into a superb all-around gymnast. Nemov has the potential to dominate men's gymnastics.

SINGLE LEG "Y" BALANCE

For this balance (right) you must have good hip flexibility and a good sense of balance – but you will also need to train hard to stay secure in this position. Begin from standing. Keep your eyes focused at one spot in front of you. Lift one leg below your groin and take hold of your heel with your hand. Lift and extend the leg.

SHOULDER STAND

Lie down with your arms by your sides. Press your arms and hands onto the mat. Bring your legs into your chest. As you do so, lift your body weight onto your shoulders (right).

HEADSTAND

Begin from a crouched position (*below left*). Point your hands and fingers forward on your mat to make the bottom of a triangular shape. Place your head at the top of the triangle to form a firm three-point balance base. Slowly curl to a tucked headstand position (*below right*). Keep the balance with a straight back. It is important not to roll your head or fall forward. When you are confident with the tucked headstand, you can straighten your legs to complete the headstand.

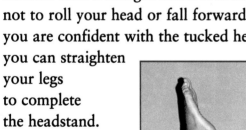

ARABESQUE

The arabesque (*center*) is an elegant one-leg balance position, which is performed by boys and girls on the floor and by girls on the beam.

Your shoulders need to be level with your hips, and the upper leg must be above the line of the shoulders. To hold an arabesque you need to have good strength in the muscles at the rear of the body and in your upper legs to hold the arched shape. Lift your head, point your toes, and extend your fingers so that every part of your body forms part of the shape.

BALANCING TIPS
It takes considerable concentration to keep your balance, particularly when the position is physically strenuous. The following tips may help.
• Make sure you are confident of your balances on the floor before attempting them on apparatus such as the beam.
• Maintain a good body line, however difficult the position, to help you to keep your balance • Try to focus your eyes on a stable base or a point in your line of vision.

"V" SIT
This is a basic balance *(left)* that can be used to develop leg and stomach strength as well as teaching you balance techniques. You begin from a simple tucked position. Use your stomach muscles as you extend your legs upward and release your arms into the "V" position. When you can perform this you can progress to even more demanding balance skills!

JAPANA FOLD
This still position is used in the floor exercise; it will also help to improve your ability to perform other more advanced movements. The Japana fold is performed with your legs at a 90° angle to each other. Fold at the hips, placing your chest on the floor, keeping your back flat. Stretch your arms out (above) *or place them by your side.*

Balances and still
POSITIONS

Balance positions, or still strength positions, are a key feature of gymnastics for boys and girls. To perform them well you must have good flexibility and strength. It can take hours of practice to develop the strength needed to lift into a particular position and then to remain steady while looking composed. Once you are confident with these positions on the floor, your coach may teach you how to perform them on different pieces of apparatus, such as the beam for girls and the rings for boys.

Moving FORWARD

Gymnastics movements such as the forward roll, the kick to handstand, and the cartwheel are the basic movements for advanced forward-moving skills. The forward roll will develop into the front somersault, and the cartwheel will become the round-off. Using a "spotter" or assistant when practicing these moves helps you to achieve a controlled and safe position and to correct any bad habits at an early stage.

ASSISTED HANDSTAND
As you kick up, your partner can hold you lightly at the hips, and at your ankles when you are in the handstand.

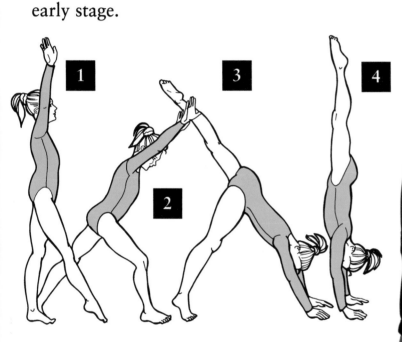

HANDSTAND
You will use the handstand on a number of pieces of apparatus, so it is important to learn it correctly. Practice an assisted handstand first *(right)*. Starting from a stretched standing position ⬛1, make a comfortable step into the lunge position, with your head up and your arms fully extended ⬛2. Lower your chest toward your front thigh, and place your hands on the floor. Gradually straighten your front leg, moving your shoulders over your hands to take the weight on your hands. Swing your top leg upward ⬛3, pushing off with your bottom leg to swing into a handstand ⬛4. As your legs arrive in the handstand position, move your shoulders backward to keep your body balanced and straight.

FORWARD ROLL

From a crouch, place your hands on the floor in front of your knees. Straighten your legs to move your body weight forward over your hands. Tuck your head between your arms. A tight tuck position with the head between the hands creates a fast rolling action (above).

IN COMPETITION
From the vault to the floor, gymnasts use a combination of forward movements in a routine, as shown left by Vitaly Scherbo (former Soviet Union). A typical exercise may include a handspring and a flyspring followed by a front somersault.

SPRINGS

These movements, often called forward accelerators, are an important part of a gymnast's routine. The kick to handstand *(see page 30)* can progress into a handspring, shown left by Vitaly Scherbo, and a flyspring *(below)*. The flyspring and the handspring are similar but in the flyspring the legs stay together.

Skilled gymnasts can increase the speed of forward movement to help them perform high and fast-rotating somersaults.

CARTWHEEL WITH 1/4 TURN

Performed sideways or facing forward (below), *this is similar to a handstand, but the first hand is placed at a 90° angle to the front foot. As the leading leg swings toward a handstand, make a quarter turn into a straddled handstand position. Press with the bottom leg; push from the hands to finish with an inward quarter turn, legs together.*

FLYSPRING

This can be performed from a handspring or a small prejump. The feet are behind the hips, the arms are raised, the chest is flat, and the knees are slightly bent. As the body leans forward, the gymnast pushes from the legs onto the hands. The heels are lifted to drive the legs over the head, and a powerful arm and shoulder push produces flight from the hands.

31

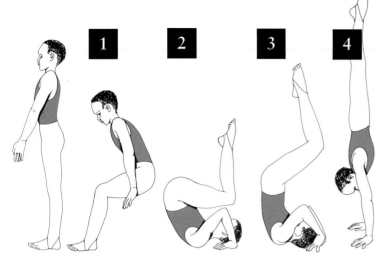

BACKWARD ROLL TO HANDSTAND

From a standing position 1, place your hands behind you; move off balance, reaching for the floor – fingers point forward. In the early stages, the legs are bent. Tuck your head in as you roll; move your hands to the floor above the shoulders – fingers point forward 2. Move your knees back toward your shoulders; extend your body 3. Your arms push you into a handstand 4.

Moving BACKWARD

A good gymnast must be able to move backward on different pieces of apparatus *(right)*, just as well as he or she does forward! Learning skills such as backward rolls and backward walkovers (always under the supervision of a qualified coach), will help you to overcome any fears about not being able to see behind you. These moves will help you learn more advanced backflips and backward somersaults.

BACKWARD WALKOVER

As the lead leg is lifted 1 the body moves forward to keep the balance on the support foot. The back is bent and the arms reach back to the floor. The lead leg is drawn upward while the support leg pushes to swing the body over the hands 2. The handstand splits 3 help control the movement before the legs are placed one at a time on the floor 4.

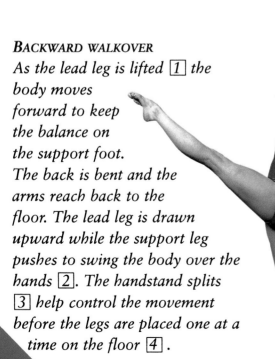

1   2   3

ROUND-OFF

The round-off, or Arab spring, is used to change forward movement into backward rotation. Step into a comfortable lunge ⬚1 . Place your first hand in front of the front foot; as your legs swing toward a handstand, rotate your second hand, placing it alongside the first hand ⬚2 . Snap your feet downward. With a strong push from your arms, your chest lifts ⬚3 Land with your feet in front of your hips ⬚4 .

BACKFLIP

Also called backward handspring, this is normally preceded by a round-off to provide backward momentum.

For a controlled and safe backflip make a dish shape (see page 10); begin to fall off balance, pivoting backward from your feet. The knees bend slightly but must not move forward.

As the body moves back, pull your shoulders quickly backward. With a strong leg push, drive your arms backward, reaching into the arched handstand position. The head should not be thrown backward. Quickly change the body shape into a dish and push vigorously from the hands. Bring your feet quickly to the floor, lifting the chest rapidly to finish the move in a dished standing position.

The sequence (left) shows a backflip.

TAKE CARE OF YOUR HANDS

As a gymnast you will place your hands under a lot of pressure. In order to withstand the heavy training, you need to toughen up the skin on your hands – without this the skin may blister and tear. Calluses can form on hard skin, and if they are not removed they may tear as you swing around the apparatus. Gymnasts use a pumice stone *(right)* to remove the calluses. Tough but smooth skin will allow you to increase the length of your training sessions.

Advanced MOVEMENTS

Many of the top gymnasts perform amazing movements, which require great courage and almost unbelievable skill. The more complex the movements, the higher the difficulty rating, and the greater the possibility of receiving bonus points in competition *(see page 23)*. A gymnast must only perform in competition those skills that he or she can perform safely and without technical faults. The advanced movements will have been developed from well-learned basic movements and will have been performed many times as individual elements before they are included in a competition routine.

Chinese Li Xuan performs a straddled Tkatchev.

GIANT SWING
The giant swing (left) *is perhaps the most important skill on the uneven bars (for girls) and the horizontal bar (for boys). The gymnast must create a great deal of momentum to completely rotate around the bar with the body in a handstand position.*

TKATCHEV
In this spectacular move the gymnast changes the direction of rotation as he or she thrusts from the bar. In the air he or she rotates forward in a half somersault to recatch the bar. This move can be performed with the legs straddled or piked.

YURCHENKO VAULT

Natalia Yurchenko, from the former Soviet Union, first perfomed this vault (below), which is now a regular feature of advanced gymnasts. The vault is preceded by a round-off to land backward on the springboard; this is followed by a back handspring onto the horse. The gymnast performs a somersault in flight from the horse.

DOUBLE-BACK SOMERSAULT

To perform the double-back somersault the gymnast must create good backward rotation from the round-off or backflip, but must also jump high enough during the takeoff. ⬜1 Once the gymnast has left the floor, a tight tuck allows for a fast spin ⬜2. Before landing the legs and body are quickly extended ⬜3 to slow down the rotation and allow the gymnast to control the landing ⬜4. Top gymnasts are able to add twists to the double somersaults.

FAME IN A NAME

Many new gymnastics movements are named for the gymnast who first performed the element in a major event.

A recent development in gymnastics is the difficult and spectacular Kovacs movement on the horizontal bar, shown right by Li Xiaoshuang from China. Kovacs, a Hungarian gymnast, first performed the double-back somersault over the bar to regrasp the bar, a move to which he gave his name.

Chinese Mo Huilan *(below)* performs a "Gaylord," named after male gymnast Mitch Gaylord (USA). This move is sometimes unofficially known as a "Mo" because she performs it so well!

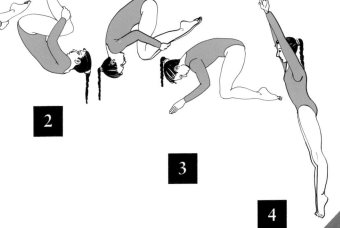

1

2

3

4

Step and lunge   *Cartwheel quarter turn*   *Spring turn*   *Round-off*

Devising a ROUTINE

Top gymnasts develop a routine over a number of years. The coach and gymnast begin to work on the basic elements of the routine, which will be performed in a "skeleton" form in competitions. When more advanced skills have been perfected, these will gradually replace the less difficult movements in the routine. Any routine must be designed to include difficult skills that the gymnast can perform safely and also satisfy the special requirements on each apparatus.

WOMEN'S ROUTINE
This is built around the series of tumbles or acrobatic skills which the gymnast can consistently perform to achieve a high start value for difficulty. The routine will contain jumps, leaps, and spins. The routine is set to music – a choreographer will work with the gymnasts to link the dynamic movements with elements of dance and interesting still positions and body movements. The illustration (above) shows part of a simple female floor exercise.

ON THE FLOOR
In competition, you must cover the whole floor area (below). Perform a difficult series of tumbles on the diagonals; perform other tumbles and linking exercises along the side.

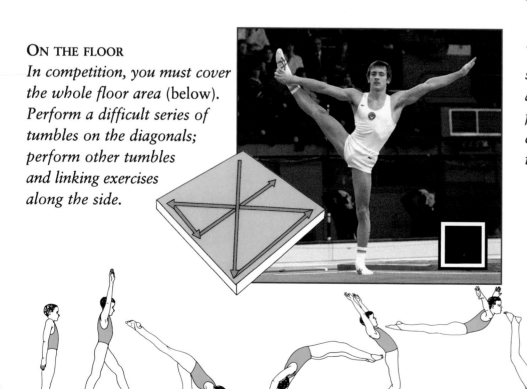

You can only move across the same diagonal or side of the area twice. Stepan Martsinkiv, from the former Soviet Union, demonstrates a "Y" balance in the floor exercise (left).

Handspring   *Dive forward roll*   *Jump turn*

Split leap   Stag leap   Pirouette   Arabesque

MUSIC
Girls have a free choice of music for the floor routine. Spend time with your coach finding a piece of music that will suit your personality and show off your qualities and talents. The music must have a range of rhythms that can match the varying pace of your moves.

BOYS' ROUTINE
This must include a series of forward and a series of backward tumbles together with a strength held part. Very complex combinations of tumbles are required to achieve a high start value for the exercise. The routine illustrated (below) is a typical basic one that would be performed by a young gymnast.

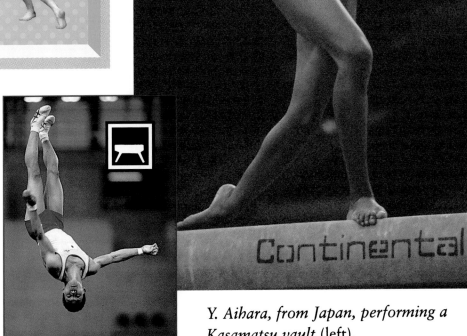

Y. Aihara, from Japan, performing a Kasamatsu vault (left).

Backward roll to handstand   Step turn   Round-off   Back flip

Safety FIRST

Your coach will ensure that you only train for and perform those movements and skills for which you have been prepared, and which are within your ability. A caring coach will always be concerned about your health and safety. If you are unwell, develop an injury, or are unhappy in any way, talk to your coach. He or she should be a friend and will wish to maintain your well-being.

A young gymnast chalks his hands during training (below).

CHALK

Use chalk, a powder of magnesium carbonate, on your hands and feet to absorb any moisture or sweat, produced during training. The chalk will help you to keep a firm grip on the apparatus, such as the bars and rings.

MATS

You and your coach must check that a safe area is created by placing suitable matting beneath or around the apparatus *(above)*.

DO'S AND DON'TS
• Always warm up before doing gymnastic exercises • Only train in the presence of a qualified coach • Only practice what you have been asked to by your coach • Wear suitable clothing
• Never wear socks on polished surfaces
• Don't wear jewelry or watches in the gym • If you are unsure about what is required of you, talk to your coach • Be observant when moving around the gym
• Don't fool around in the gym • Always try your hardest • Enjoy your training!

Your hair should be neatly groomed or tied back (left) *to keep it away from your eyes and to prevent it from becoming caught in any apparatus.*

Glossary

Arch
A basic gymnastics body shape.

Body line
The body shape made by the gymnast.

Body tension
Keeping the tension on specific muscles.

Choreography
The arrangement of movements in a dance or routine.

Contract
To tighten a muscle.

Difficulty rating
The system in competition according to which the difficulty of a movement is judged.

Dish
A basic gymnastics body shape.

Dismount
A move used to take you off a piece of apparatus.

Dynamic
A powerful movement or action.

Elements
Gymnastic skills or moves.

Endurance
The ability to repeatedly perform exercises before tiring.

Extend
To stretch and reach.

Flexibility
The range of movement in a joint of the body.

Forward accelerators
Moves which help to increase the speed of forward movement.

Joint
The point where two bones meet.

Momentum
The force of motion gained in movement.

Mount
The way a gymnast gets on a piece of apparatus.

Muscle
Those parts of the body that help us move.

Pike
A position in which the legs are bent at the hips to create a "V" shape.

Posture
Your body stance or position.

Rotatation
A movement in which the body turns.

Routine
A complete series of movements.

Special requirement
In competition, specific movements required in a routine.

Spotting
Support from a partner or coach.

Squat
A move in which the knees and hips are bent to bring the knees between the arms.

Start value
The score from which points are subtracted to give the final result.

Straddle
A position in which the legs are wide apart.

Tense
To tightena muscle.

Tuck
A position in which the knees are held into the chest.

Warm-up
Preparing the body for exercise.

Key to apparatus

Floor *Rings* *Parallel bars* *Pommel horse* *Uneven bars*   *Horizontal bar*   *Vault*   *Beam*

Index

Photo Credits: *Abbreviations: t-top, m-middle, b-bottom, r-right, l-left*

All photos by Roger Vlitos except for: front cover, 6, 10t, 14m, 16t & b, 19ml & b, 20b, 21tr, 22t & m both, 26t & 37m – Frank Spooner; 4-5, 7t, 15t, 16ml & mr; 17t, 18tl & m & b all, 20m all, 21tl & b, 22b, 23tl & br, 24bl, 25m & b, 27b, 31 both, 32t, 34l &35 all – Supersport/Eileen Langsley; 28bl – Mike Weinstock; 7bl & br – Mary Evans Picture Library; 14-15, 18tr, 20-21, 27t, 36, 37tr & back cover – Rex Features.

Models supplied by Stoke-on-Trent Gymnastics Centre *(apart from page 30).*
The publishers would like to thank the staff and gymnasts at the Stoke-on-Trent Gymnastics Centre and the staff at the headquarters of the British Gymnastics Association for their help and co-operation in the preparation of this book.